# JUANITA'S STATUE

*Anne García-Romero*

**BROADWAY PLAY PUBLISHING INC**
224 E 62nd St, NY, NY 10065
www.broadwayplaypub.com
info@broadwayplaypub.com

JUANITA'S STATUE
© Copyright 2013 by Anne García-Romero

First printing: March 2013
I S B N: 978-0-88145-562-5

Book design: Marie Donovan
Page make-up: Adobe Indesign
Typeface: Palatino
Printed and bound in the U S A

JUANITA'S STATUE was originally commissioned and developed by the Joseph Papp Public Theater/New York Shakespeare Festival, George C Wolfe, Producer.

The development of JUANITA'S STATUE was also supported by a fellowship from the Jerome Foundation through the Playwrights' Center of Minneapolis.

JUANITA'S STATUE was part of the Jungle Theater Playreading Series, Minneapolis, and the Voices! Reading series at Hartford Stage and The Ford Theatre Foundation's Latino Playreading Series in Los Angeles.

JUANITA'S STATUE was originally presented in a workshop on 6 December 1999 at NYSF/Public Theater with the following cast and creative contributors:

JUANITA ........................................................Camillia Sanes
CARMELA............................................... Vanessa Aspillaga
DON JUAN ...........................................................Gary Perez
Ensemble ...... Al Espinosa, Denise Casano, Lázaro Perez,
Paula Pizzi

Director ...................................................... Leah C Gardiner

JUANITA'S STATUE received its world premiere on 3 March 2012 at Nevada Repertory Company, (Rob Gander, Producer) with the following cast and creative contributors:

| | |
|---|---|
| JUANITA | Sarah Rodriguez |
| CARMELA | Melissa Ortiz |
| IGNACIO | J J von Nolde |
| BEATRÍZ/ELENA | Jessica Mann |
| ALEJANDRA/DOÑA LOLA | Christy Markwell |
| TOMÁS/HUCKSTER | Dean Bart-Plange |
| DON PEDRO/DON JUAN | James Schlauch |
| DOÑA ALMA/ROSA/LEONORA | Audrey Brown |
| EDWINA/ACTIVISTA | Breana Edgerton |
| HORTENSIA | Ashley Gong |
| MANUEL | Anthony Mendoza |
| RUFINO/EDUARDO | Jason Bunales |
| *Director* | Stacey Spain |
| *Set, lighting & sound design* | Michael Fernbach |
| *Costume design* | Monica Fritcher |

# ACKNOWLEDGMENTS

Special thanks to: Susan Gurman, Shirley Fishman, Leah C. Gardiner, Juliette Carrillo, Rob Gander, Stacey Spain, the Jerome Foundation, The Playwrights' Center of Minneapolis, Megan Monaghan-Rivas, Jeremy Cohen, Lizzet Alvarez, Barbara, Alicia, Toño and Mercedes García-Romero.

# CHARACTERS

JUANITA DE LA CRUZ, *20s*
CARMELA, *20s,* JUANITA'*s best friend*
STATUE OF DON JUAN TENORIO, *40s, a stone statue*
IGNACIO, *20, suave, society boy*
HORTENSIA, *15,* IGNACIO'*s sister*
DON PEDRO, *late 40s,* IGNACIO'*s father*
DOÑA ALMA, *late 40s,* IGNACIO'*s mother*
ALEJANDRA, *40s, wealthy art collector*
MANUEL, *mid-40s,* ALEJANDRA'*s husband*
EDUARDO, *mid-20s, savvy businessman,* ALEJANDRA'*s son*
EDWINA, *20, savvy businesswoman,* ALEJANDRA'*s
    daughter*
TOMÁS, *late 20s, biker*
RUFINO, *early 40s, biker,* TOMÁS'*s lover*
LEONORA, *early 40s, biker,* ELENA'*s lover*
ELENA, *25, biker,* TOMÁS'*s friend*
BEATRÍZ, *18, innocent, society bride*
DOÑA LOLA, *early 40s,* BEATRÍZ'*s mother, matron of honor*
HUCKSTER, *20s, bright, cheery street vendor*
ACTIVISTA, *20s, loud, urban radical*
ROSA, *40s, sage-like street vendor*

*Setting: The cityscape of a Spanglish-speaking land*

Note: This play is inspired by the comedies of the Spanish Golden Age. The performance style of this play ought to be one of heightened realism, bordering on farce/commedia. The roles need not be played solely naturalistically. In addition, all roles can be cast multi-culturally.

This play can be cast with twelve actors playing the twenty roles. The casting could be:

JUANITA DE LA CRUZ
CARMELA
IGNACIO
HORTENSIA
DON PEDRO/STATUE OF DON JUAN TENORIO
DOÑA ALMA/LEONORA/ROSA
TOMÁS/HUCKSTER
ALEJANDRA/DOÑA LOLA
BEATRÍZ/ELENA
EDWINA/ACTIVISTA
MANUEL
RUFINO/EDUARDO

for Barbara and Mercedes

(*Lights rise on* IGNACIO's *bedroom in a wealthy city district. Evening.* JUANITA, *in a cherry red sleeveless dress, barefoot, kneels up on his bed.* IGNACIO, *in an untucked, white dress shirt, slacks, barefoot, stands next to the bed.*)

JUANITA: Screw honor.

IGNACIO: Sí, Juanita…because an amazing new adventure awaits us.

JUANITA: Is that what you tell all the chicas?

IGNACIO: In my dreams, you appear…

JUANITA: Really.

IGNACIO: submerged in the sea, your cherry red dress swirling…

JUANITA: I do love to swim in the sea.

IGNACIO: caressing your lovely legs…

JUANITA: Go on…

IGNACIO: clinging to your brilliant breasts…

JUANITA: More, por favor…

IGNACIO: Your heavenly hair floating around…

(IGNACIO *runs his fingers through* JUANITA's *hair.*)

IGNACIO: uncovering your erotic ears. Bueno, mi amor.

JUANITA: Ignacio…I…ay, ay, ay. But. Wait. So there's no conflict of interest here between desire and honor?

IGNACIO: I'm honored to desire you. No conflict.

JUANITA: What about the code?

IGNACIO: I don't believe in codes.

JUANITA: So you absolutely do not believe in the code of honor which separates you from me in order to protect your name, standing and future in this city?

IGNACIO: *(Laying it on thick)* Every day since we met at the restaurant in the park when you served me piping hot cafecitos, I lie here seeing you in my dreams, submerged in the sea, your cherry red dress swirling as you beckon to me and I swim forward eagerly.

JUANITA: Ignacio?

IGNACIO: Sí, mi amor?

JUANITA: Screw honor.

*(IGNACIO and JUANITA kiss and fall into bed as lights shift.)*

*(Lights rise on DON PEDRO, DOÑA ALMA and HORTENSIA in the parlor.)*

HORTENSIA: She wore a sleeveless dress the color of bright cherries.

DON PEDRO: Por favor.

DOÑA ALMA: Que tacky.

HORTENSIA: Que sí. Yesterday she served us cafecitos in the park restaurante. Then later we saw her in the park laughing with some female friend. And she walked right up to Ignacio.

DOÑA ALMA: Ay madre mia, he talked to a girl from the other side of the river?!

HORTENSIA: Who crawls into this city each day to try to improve her position in life.

DON PEDRO: Bueno, la pobre, if she was born on that side of the river she will marry some poor fool who shovels coal for a living or fills some man's glass with wine.

HORTENSIA: But you should have seen how Ignacio's eyes widened, Papi. And then she winked her eye. Ay Papi, he looked so…so…happy it was revolting.

DOÑA ALMA: Ay the gossip, the scandal!

HORTENSIA: If mis amigas saw her talking to us, no friend will talk to me for a week, a month, maybe a year and then no boy will ever like me and I'll end up una vieja, single, an old, eternally lonely lady.

DON PEDRO: But Ignacio is going to marry Beatriz. They will live a life of leisure and prosperity and one day, he will inherit her family's fortune. No woman will threaten the honor of mi familia.

DOÑA ALMA: I tried to raise him properly, to desire his own kind and stay within his own circle.

DON PEDRO: His eyes may wander but never more than that. His honor will remain intact.

HORTENSIA: But Papi, what if he sees her again? What if someone who knows about the wedding sees him flirting with her? How can we stop the idle gossip that will be the downfall of our very lives?

DON PEDRO: He'll never risk losing his reputation. Mi Ignacio is quite intelligent.

DOÑA ALMA: And quite handsome.

HORTENSIA: But so horny!

DON PEDRO: His mind may wander but his body will not.

DOÑA ALMA & HORTENSIA: Of course.

DON PEDRO: Que sí.

HORTENSIA: Ignaciooooooo…

(HORTENSIA *exits running as lights shift.*)

(*Lights rise on* IGNACIO *and* JUANITA *sitting up in bed, in each others arms, wearing underwear only, kissing as*

HORTENSIA *Barges in on them.* IGNACIO *breaks away from* JUANITA *in horror at being discovered.* HORTENSIA *gasps.)*

HORTENSIA: I have seen the dawn of infamy.

IGNACIO: Hortensia, OUT.

HORTENSIA: In the park, with your eyes is one thing. But in your bed, with your hands and your lips and... and your...tongue...is another.

IGNACIO: I order you to leave.

HORTENSIA: You can't order me like Papi. Wait until he sees you're in bed with...with...

JUANITA: Juanita...encantada.

(JUANITA *goes to give* HORTENSIA *a customary greeting, a kiss on the cheek.* HORTENSIA *recoils.)*

HORTENSIA: I don't talk to or touch your kind.

JUANITA: My kind?

HORTENSIA: Roaming the streets unaccompanied. A decent woman never leaves her house alone.

IGNACIO: Hortensia...

HORTENSIA: Trying to improve her position in life by robbing the honor of this familia.

IGNACIO: Out...

HORTENSIA: My parents, Don Pedro and Doña Alma, will not allow it.

IGNACIO: Now...

HORTENSIA: I'm Papi's favorita and even more so now.

JUANITA: Cálmate.

HORTENSIA: You've stolen my brother away from us.

JUANITA: I don't steal.

HORTENSIA: He's familia. He's ours. And he's getting married tomorrow and you will not escape from this hideous crime.

IGNACIO: Out.

HORTENSIA: Papi? Paaapppiiii? Pppaaaaapppiiiii! *(She exits running.)*

JUANITA: Getting married?

IGNACIO: Juanita...

JUANITA: Mañana?

IGNACIO: Sí.

JUANITA: I'm outta here.

IGNACIO: But it's not what you think.

JUANITA: Don't you even tell me what I think.

IGNACIO: I'll explain...

JUANITA: No explanation necessary...

IGNACIO: But...you have to leave.

JUANITA: Gladly.

IGNACIO: Now.

*(JUANITA begins to gather her clothing.)*

IGNACIO: If mi papá finds you in here his eyes will bulge. His cheeks will turn the color of bricks. His teeth will grind with growling ferocity. His palms will rise and fall striking random household objects. He will banish me to solitary confinement. He will tarnish your reputation forever if he doesn't kill you first.

JUANITA: Kill me? First?

*(IGNACIO nods. JUANITA bolts toward the door. IGNACIO blocks her.)*

IGNACIO: Not the door. Quick, out the window!

*(IGNACIO and JUANITA run to the window as lights shift.)*

*(Lights rise on* DON PEDRO *and* DOÑA ALMA *sitting in the parlor. She knits while he reads the newspaper.)*

DOÑA ALMA: Ay, our son's wedding fiesta. We'll feast on the freshest fish, wonderful wines and a colossal, caramelized, coconut cake.

DON PEDRO: Sí, mi alma.

DOÑA ALMA: The city's finest familias will sit at elegant tables toasting our son. And then we'll dance gracefully to la música of guitars and violins.

DON PEDRO: Claro, mi alma.

DOÑA ALMA: And we'll be written up in the society pages and people will talk about this fiesta for years.

*(*HORTENSIA *enters running.)*

HORTENSIA: Papi!

DOÑA ALMA: Hortensia, lower your voice in front of your papá.

HORTENSIA: But Papi, she's here and…they were and… he is and…we won't…

DON PEDRO: *(Correcting her)* Hortensia, speak clearly.

HORTENSIA: But that girl I was telling you about…she's here.

DOÑA ALMA: Ay por Dios!

*(*DON PEDRO *puts down his newspaper.)*

HORTENSIA: In Ignacio's bed.

DOÑA ALMA: A harlot in my house?

DON PEDRO: Your brother has that girl from the other side of the river in his bed?

HORTENSIA: He does. And they were doing nasty, ugly things that rob our house of its honor.

*(*DOÑA ALMA *lets out a scream.)*

DOÑA ALMA: Ay the wedding, ay our plans, ay our lives.

DON PEDRO: *(To* HORTENSIA*)* Where are they?

HORTENSIA: Lying together in his room. O Papi, the infamy.

DON PEDRO: No woman will threaten the honor of my house.

HORTENSIA: I saw bare flesh.

DOÑA ALMA: How horrible!

DON PEDRO: I will drag this woman out into the street and denounce her and her familia. No one threatens the honor of my house. *(To* DOÑA ALMA*)* This is your fault. You're too liberal with him.

DOÑA ALMA: *(To* DON PEDRO*)* This is your fault. You're too strict with him.

HORTENSIA: Come on, Papi.

DON PEDRO: Ignacio. Ignacio!

DOÑA ALMA: Save our son. Save our plans. Save our lives.

*(*HORTENSIA *exits with* DON PEDRO *following her as lights shift.)*

*(Lights rise on* IGNACIO *and* JUANITA *at the window.)*

JUANITA: *(Looking out the window)* Ay three stories down!

IGNACIO: Okay. The door, then.

*(They run to the door.)*

DON PEDRO: *(Off stage getting closer)* IGNACIO!

IGNACIO: My future…

JUANITA: My health…

IGNACIO: My inheritance…

JUANITA: My life…

DON PEDRO: *(Off stage, getting very close)* IGNACIO!!

IGNACIO: My life…

JUANITA: My death!

*(IGNACIO grabs a shirt of his and tosses it to JUANITA.)*

IGNACIO: Quick. Put it on.

JUANITA: Your ivory silk shirt?

IGNACIO: So you can slide past the siege.

*(IGNACIO tosses JUANITA a pair of his slacks.)*

JUANITA: Your slick wool slacks?

IGNACIO: To provide a path through the panic.

*(IGNACIO tosses JUANITA a jacket.)*

JUANITA: Your gentleman's jacket?!

IGNACIO: To swiftly smooth your shape.

*(IGNACIO tosses JUANITA a pair of his shoes.)*

JUANITA: Your lovely leather wingtips?!

IGNACIO: So you can take flight.

*(IGNACIO tosses JUANITA a hat, which she puts on hiding her hair.)*

JUANITA: Your truly fashionable fedora?!

IGNACIO: Stylishly steadfast for the sake of our lives. *(Beat)* Maybe my fancy and honorable wardrobe will save us from destruction.

JUANITA: *(Praying)* "If wearing these clothes can disguise me as one so high and mighty…oh Heaven, let them perform their transformation on me.»

*(JUANITA takes her dress and shoes and throws them out the window. IGNACIO quickly makes the bed and throws on some wrinkled clothing.)*

DON PEDRO: *(Off stage, very close)* IGNACIO!

JUANITA: Cards. Quick.

*(IGNACIO grabs a pack of cards.)*

IGNACIO: *(Incredulous)* Hey, you're a damn fine dude in my duds.

*(IGNACIO and JUANITA sit on the bed and begin playing cards as DON PEDRO and HORTENSIA burst into the room.)*

HORTENSIA: She was just here. But…he…wasn't.

IGNACIO: This is…mi amigo…

JUANITA: Juan. It's a pleasure, señor, señorita.

*(JUANITA shakes DON PEDRO's hand and then gives HORTENSIA a kiss on both cheeks which she instantly enjoys.)*

HORTENSIA: *(Suddenly smitten)* The pleasure's all mine.

DON PEDRO: Where's the woman?

*(HORTENSIA stares at JUAN as DON PEDRO continues.)*

DON PEDRO: Ignacio, did the two of you have some low class lady under my roof? Tell me now son.

IGNACIO: Papá, we've been playing cards all evening.

HORTENSIA: But, I saw them lying in bed together, bare flesh and everything…but *(To JUANITA/JUAN)* you weren't here before, were you?

DON PEDRO: Bueno?

JUANITA: Que sí, I've been enjoying an enchanting evening with mi compañero, Ignacio, a fine player and lover of…cards.

IGNACIO: Hortensia you were fantasizing again.

DON PEDRO: Hortensia?

HORTENSIA: Pero, Papi, I swear, it was the girl with the cherry dress from the park. Could I have been fantasizing?

(DON PEDRO *searches the room.*)

HORTENSIA: *(Looking at* JUANITA/JUAN, *to herself)* If I'm fantasizing right now, don't wake me, por favor.

DON PEDRO: *(To* JUANITA*)* My son is lying to me. Where's this woman?!

IGNACIO: *(Distracting* DON PEDRO*)* She escaped out the window.

(DON PEDRO *runs to the window.*)

DON PEDRO: A dress and shoes on the street.

(DON PEDRO *grabs* IGNACIO *by the hair.*)

DON PEDRO: I will find this woman who jeopardizes your position in society and when I do, I will make sure she can never lift her head or lips or legs in this city again.

IGNACIO: *(In pain)* Ay Papá.

DON PEDRO: If word gets out you were screwing a low class harlot the night before your wedding, the bride's family is so refined…so religious that they will call it off, you will not be married, you will never inherit their fortune and our family name will be ruined forever. No woman will rob this house of its honor and live to see her honor unscathed. And you will not leave this house again. You are marrying Beatríz tomorrow. Entiendes?

IGNACIO: *(Meekly)* Sí, Papá.

DON PEDRO: Eh?

IGNACIO: *(More audibly)* Sí, Papá.

DON PEDRO: What is her name?

IGNACIO: Por favor, Papá.

(DON PEDRO *grabs* IGNACIO's *hair again.*)

DON PEDRO: Her name!

IGNACIO: Juanita.

DON PEDRO: Despicable name. Why did you do this?

IGNACIO: *(Softly)* Por favor, Papá.

DON PEDRO: Eh?!

IGNACIO: *(With a burst)* Because she's incredible, different than any other woman. She's noble, intelligent, beautiful, charismatic and kind. I don't want to marry Beatríz.

DON PEDRO: You will marry Beatríz. You will improve our standing in society. This little adventure will not ruin the reputation of your familia.

IGNACIO: Papá, por favor.

DON PEDRO: If our reputation is ruined, society señoras will stop talking to your Mamá at fiestas and no man will even glance at Hortensia.

HORTENSIA: Not even Juan?

DON PEDRO: Hortensia! Don't interrupt me.

HORTENSIA: *(To* IGNACIO*)* What's Juan's last name?

DON PEDRO: Hortensia!

HORTENSIA: Sí, Papa.

DON PEDRO: Don't either of you care about the honor of *our* house?!

HORTENSIA & IGNACIO: Sí, Papa.

JUANITA: *(Lying)* Señor, I assure you that Ignacio is a most honorable hombre.

DON PEDRO: Don't interrupt me, or try to convince me of my son's innocence. Vete, go home and don't ever bother returning to my house again.

(JUANITA/JUAN *leaves as* HORTENSIA *and* IGNACIO *look after him/her, totally smitten.*)

JUANITA: Adios señores y señorita.

HORTENSIA & IGNACIO: Adios Juan.

(JUANITA *exits running.*)

DON PEDRO: Hortensia! Ignacio!

HORTENSIA & IGNACIO: Sí, Papá!

DON PEDRO: Do you care about the honor of *our* house above all else?!

HORTENSIA & IGNACIO: Sí, Papá!

DON PEDRO: What did you say?

HORTENSIA & IGNACIO: SÍ, PAPÁ!

(IGNACIO *starts running.*)

IGNACIO: Juanita...Juanita...Juaniiiittttaaaaaaa. *(He exits running.)*

DON PEDRO: Ignacio. Ignacio, come back, now, right now, ahora mismo. I order you...Ignacio... You are going to help me find that Juanita woman and when I do, she'll be lucky if she can still walk let alone screw. Ignacio...

(DON PEDRO *runs after* IGNACIO *and exits as* DOÑA ALMA *enters.*)

HORTENSIA: *(Calling after* IGNACIO*)* What's Juan's last naaaaame?

DOÑA ALMA: Did Papi save our lives from ruin? Pedro? Ignacio?

HORTENSIA: Ay Mami, I saw groping hands, fingers, tongues, bare flesh and at first it scared me.

DOÑA ALMA: Where's my son? Where's the husband-to-be?

HORTENSIA: But then I met Juan…and somewhere below my belly…deep down there I think I'm beginning to understand.

DOÑA ALMA: Where's your papá?

HORTENSIA: Mami, down there creates craziness.

IGNACIO: *(Offstage)* Juanitaaaaaaaaa.

DON PEDRO: *(Offstage)* Ignacio, Ignacio, ven aqui, Ignacio…

*(DOÑA ALMA runs to the window and looks out.)*

DOÑA ALMA: Mi familia running through the streets… what will people say? Ay por dios.

HORTENSIA: And this craziness is something we can't control. Ay Juan.

DOÑA ALMA: Ay the wedding. Ay our plans. Ay our lives. Pedro? Pedro! Ignacio? Ignacio! Ignacio!

*(DOÑA ALMA exits running. HORTENSIA Runs to the window.)*

HORTENSIA: JUAAAAAAAAAAAAAAAAAN!

*(Lights shift.)*

*(The next morning. A park in the business district. Lights rise on JUANITA and CARMELA standing next to a statue of Don Juan. JUANITA is still dressed in IGNACIO's clothing.)*

CARMELA: *(Reading inscription)* "Don Juan Tenorio. He thought he had plenty of time to pay for his sins but he paid with his life."

JUANITA: What kind of city do we live in where a woman dresses like this to protect herself from men like him?

CARMELA: You wanna be my boyfriend for a day dressed like that?

JUANITA: Just for one day.

CARMELA: You're not my type.

JUANITA: Puh-lease, for your favorita-best-friend-since-we-were-three?

CARMELA: In bed with a rich boy from the city?

JUANITA: Ay, he seduced me.

CARMELA: Like last week's Iván.

JUANITA: Sexy yet sergeant-like.

CARMELA: And before that Estéban.

JUANITA: Dashing yet difficult.

CARMELA: And now there's incredible Ignacio who's getting married. Right. Real swift, chica.

JUANITA: He didn't tell me.

CARMELA: So you sleep with a rich husband-to-be, his papá chases after you to avenge his family's honor and you want me to pose as your girlfriend until his papi loses your trail? *(Beat)* Por favor. Two catering gigs in one day. I don't have time for this. I've gotta go get ready for work.

JUANITA: Take me with you. Come on...last Tuesday, I covered for you so you could escape your catastrophic catering life and gallivant across the park with that hot boy from the university.

CARMELA: *(Recalling fondly)* Ah, yes, the one who was studying wildlife mating patterns, promised to call, but didn't.

JUANITA: But for that one night...

CARMELA: He was very wild and not so studious. *(Beat)* Ay no, Juanita.

JUANITA: But Don Pedro had violence in his eyes. This is a man who literally destroys lives for the sake of his own familia.

CARMELA: *(Looking at statue)* Like Don Juan Tenorio who destroyed reputations and lives...

JUANITA: *(Pleading)* ...for the sake of his own pleasure, except he lived hundreds of years ago and Don Pedro is running through the city trying to kill me as we speak.

CARMELA: *(Looking at the statue)* Maybe he's just a character some old priest created to warn women about the "evil men" who want to seduce us. I mean if he did live, why was he a serial seducer? Privilege?

JUANITA: Possibly.

CARMELA: Power?

JUANITA: Probably.

CARMELA: Overactive cojones?

JUANITA: Positively.

CARMELA: The basic urge few can truly suppress. Yet women did desire him.

JUANITA: Some more than others. *(Beat)* Society señoritas, fisherwomen, brides, he tricked them all and then...

CARMELA: Then the statue of one señorita's dead father seeks revenge...

JUANITA: His stone hand grabs Don Juan's hand and hurls the trickster into the burning flames of hell. Adios.

CARMELA: So if Don Pedro is like the avenging statue trying to kill you, then you are like...

JUANITA: *(Pointing to the statue of Don Juan)* But I'm not like him. Absolutely not. No way, señorita. Que no.

CARMELA: Alright. Alright.

JUANITA: I'm more enlightened than that, Carmela.

CARMELA: But do some chicas or chicos still want some version of the Don Juan ways?

JUANITA: Maybe some. But not me.

CARMELA: But what if there were no more Don Juan period, just obliteration, kaboom, fin?

JUANITA: Or...what if there were a new Don Juan who takes care of our profound need for pleasure?

CARMELA: And passion...

JUANITA: But with devotion not dominance.

CARMELA: Breaking the patriarchal pattern so we can find...

JUANITA: Love with no lying nor leaving.

CARMELA: Impossible.

JUANITA: We can only hope. *(Beat)* How do I look?

CARMELA: Like one sad señor.

JUANITA: How do I walk? *(She practices walking.)*

CARMELA: Like a silly señorita.

*(JUANITA practices walking again.)*

CARMELA: Like some mad machista. *(Beat)* I don't believe there can be any new Don Juan ways.

JUANITA: What if I show you? Let me be your new Don Juan for the day, eh?

CARMELA: *(Rolling her eyes)* So I can learn the power of true love?

JUANITA: Ay I can't go home. I can't stay here. At these fiestas, you'll cater and I'll keep you company. So then let me, the new Juan, escort you, the lovely Carmela with utmost respect and honor.

CARMELA: Screw honor. You're making me late.

*(HUCKSTER enters and approaches them.)*

HUCKSTER: Yo mister!

JUANITA: *(To* CARMELA*)* Mister?

HUCKSTER: You and your girlfriend need this book.

JUANITA: *(To* CARMELA*)* Mister? Girlfriend? These threads weave their spell. *(To* HUCKSTER*)* What book is that?

HUCKSTER: *(Cheery, non-stop)* So glad you asked because you two look so deliriously joyful together that I am completely convinced you desire my book one hundred and one love positions for life and for one low low price and everyone's buyin' 'em folks you will receive titillating information steamy inspiration and might I add otherworldly sensation so you can continue to keep things creative and kinky with your sexy mamacita mi amigo ah yes guaranteed fun fun fun for seconds minutes hours days on end with love, love and more love, lovah. Ya dig? Complete with full color diagrams.

CARMELA & JUANITA: Full color diagrams?!

JUANITA: How much?

HUCKSTER: For you, the seduction special. Slap me five.

*(*JUANITA *gives* HUCKSTER *five coins. He sells her the book.* CARMELA *grabs it and begins flipping through it in amazement.)*

DON PEDRO: *(Note: This line should be amplified so that the voice seems to be coming from everywhere. This should be done every time this line occurs throughout the play, regardless of which characters speak this line. Offstage)* JUANITA, JUANITA, JUANITA!

JUANITA: Don Pedro!

CARMELA: We're outta here.

*(*CARMELA *and* JUANITA *run off.)*

JUANITA: Gracias, señor.

HUCKSTER: Remember love love love, lovah!

(HUCKSTER *exits. Lights shift.*)

*(A garish townhouse in the arts district. Later that afternoon. Lights rise on* ALEJANDRA, *a tipsy socialite art collector, pacing in front of a contemporary painting.* MANUEL, *her even tipsier husband, and* EDUARDO *and* EDWINA, *their children, stand beside her.* ALEJANDRA *and* MANUEL *get progressively more intoxicated throughout the scene.)*

ALEJANDRA: *(Tipsy)* I spend millions collecting the finest, hip and thoroughly modern masterpieces and I am fabulously famous for it and yet no one at my own cocktail party even appreciates me. *(To* MANUEL*)* You married me for my money. *(To her children)* And my children want my wealth for their latest business scheme. They care more for money than their own mamá.

EDUARDO: We care for you.

EDWINA: We do.

EDUARDO: We love you.

EDWINA: And your money.

EDUARDO: All your twenty six hundred and seventy seven million.

EDWINA: Twenty seven hundred and seventy six million, hermano.

EDUARDO: Of course, hermana. We love both.

EDWINA: Equally.

MANUEL: *(Tipsy)* So do I.

ALEJANDRA: When will I receive the artistic appreciation and sensual satisfaction I deserve?

EDWINA: We love you, Mami.

EDUARDO: Your masterpieces and your money.

MANUEL: Of course we do.

(CARMELA *enters carrying a tray of martinis.* JUANITA *follows closely behind her, trying to fit in.*)

CARMELA: Care for another martini, señor? señora?

ALEJANDRA: *(Re:* CARMELA*)* Now here's someone who understands my needs.

(ALEJANDRA *and* MANUEL *suck down martinis.* ALEJANDRA *spots* JUANITA.*)*

ALEJANDRA: *(Re:* JUANITA*)* Ay por favor, who's that handsome hunk of flesh? *(To* JUANITA*)* What's your name, handsome?

JUANITA: De la Cruz. Juan. De la Cruz.

MANUEL: *(More tipsy)* De la Cruz? The ambassador's son?

ALEJANDRA: He looks diplomatic, doesn't he?

JUANITA: *(Pleasantly surprised)* Oh…sí. *(Going along with the ruse)* My father and I just returned from a…a diplomatic…journey.

ALEJANDRA: Your father an ambassador and you land at my cocktail party. Fabulous. Continue, cariño.

MANUEL: We didn't invite the son of the ambassador to our party? Did we?

JUANITA: My girlfriend…brought me along. I hope you don't mind. She lives…just around the corner. She came with us too…on our voyage to explore kingdoms, meet royalty and discover treasures.

ALEJANDRA: Ah young love on the high seas. Fabulous. To be treated with kindness, respect, cherished. To be in love again.

(MANUEL *hands her another martini. He drinks another too.*)

MANUEL: I respect you, lovey. Have another.

ALEJANDRA: My days of admirers are long gone
and now all I have are my children and husband
surrounding me so they can suck away my money.

EDUARDO: Mamá is obsessed with the fact that we want
her wealth.

EDWINA: Which we do for our latest business venture.
We invest money and make her

EDUARDO: and us

EDUARDO & EDWINA: gargantuan profits.

EDUARDO: We're financial wizards.

EDWINA: We like to reap bountiful benefits by investing
mamá's

EDUARDO: and other people's

EDWINA: money in stocks, bonds, futures, the open
market, we analyze numbers, we keep records, we like
making money.

EDUARDO: Money is not the root of all evil, you know.

ALEJANDRA: It's the root of all evil children.

EDWINA: But I'm your favorita.

EDUARDO: I'm her favorito.

EDWINA: I doubled our dividends.

EDUARDO: I tripled our treasury. (To JUANITA) Do you
like investing?

EDWINA: (To JUANITA) I could invest your money.

EDUARDO & EDWINA: It's our job.

EDWINA: We create more.

JUANITA: How much more?

EDUARDO: Mountains more. I'll make you richer. Ker-
ching. Ker-ching.

JUANITA: Maybe you could. My father and I brought back gold, silver and platinum...coins from distant shores.

ALEJANDRA: Such the exotic traveler.

JUANITA: We met kings and queens, reyes y reinas, maharajahs and madames...but you, señora, are by far the most radiant of them all.

ALEJANDRA: And such an intelligent young man.

MANUEL: *(Even more tipsy)* Enough with the young sexy man! Drink!

ALEJANDRA: Tell me, did you visit the museums, galleries, expositions...please talk to me about the art.

JUANITA: I saw masterpieces of modern art, massive murals, towering statues...but they don't even compare to your beauty.

(ALEJANDRA *approaches* JUANITA.)

ALEJANDRA: Take off your jacket and stay a while.

CARMELA: Excuse me. Juan is it? I think that's your girlfriend over there waving to you on her way out the door.

ALEJANDRA: Good. Let her leave.

(ALEJANDRA *grabs onto* JUANITA's *jacket.*)

JUANITA: You long for freedom, señora.

ALEJANDRA: I do.

(ALEJANDRA *clutches onto* JUANITA's *arm.*)

JUANITA: To be seen as the strong youthful woman that you are.

ALEJANDRA: He thinks I'm youthful!

CARMELA: Juanito...

(ALEJANDRA *clutches onto* JUANITA's *other arm, grabs onto her jacket.*)

JUANITA: To know that others love you in spite of the riches you possess.

ALEJANDRA: Tell me more, Juanito.

MANUEL: *(To* ALEJANDRA*)* He's really too young for you. Please, have another drink!

EDWINA: She likes him.

EDUARDO: He likes her. And her money.

EDWINA: I'm her favorite.

EDUARDO: She likes me better.

CARMELA: Juanito, I think your girlfriend's left without you.

*(*JUANITA *takes* ALEJANDRA*'s hand off her jacket and holds it in hers.)*

JUANITA: Your youthful spirit longs to soar as you are acknowledged for your talent, for your beauty, for your kindness and nothing else.

ALEJANDRA: What a wise young thing you are.

JUANITA: Soaring free from your children and husband who descend upon you for your money not motherhood or matrimony.

ALEJANDRA: Oh sí.

EDUARDO: He's annoying me.

EDWINA: He's lying.

EDUARDO: He's using wily words

EDWINA: So he can crawl inside her clothes and win her wealth.

EDUARDO: Not so fast, amigo.

ALEJANDRA: Let him speak.

*(*JUANITA *holds* ALEJANDRA*'s hands.)*

JUANITA: Your eyes perceive subjects which long to be known.

ALEJANDRA: O sí, your words awaken my mind.

JUANITA: Your hands collect paintings priceless and powerful.

ALEJANDRA: Ay sí, your perception arouses my soul.

JUANITA: But your inner value, señora, soars and surpasses all of this.

(ALEJANDRA *suddenly tries to kiss* JUANITA. MANUEL *pulls* JUANITA *away.*)

MANUEL: (*To* JUANITA) Leave. Now. (*To* ALEJANDRA) There will be no kissing of young punks at this party! Que no!

ALEJANDRA: Please let him stay!

(EDUARDO *and* EDWINA *grab hold of* ALEJANDRA.)

EDUARDO: You've aroused our mamá.

EDWINA: She will now run around this house ranting and raving for three days.

EDUARDO, EDWINA & MANUEL: And then maybe no one will get her money.

(MANUEL *begins to usher* JUANITA *out.*)

ALEJANDRA: Let go of him.

EDWINA: Mamá, you must relax.

EDUARDO: Calmate.

ALEJANDRA: Didn't you hear what he said? I need to soar! We must soar together Juan.

CARMELA: Juan, time to leave now.

ALEJANDRA: Speak your wise words so together we can soar.

MANUEL: Out. Now. (*To* CARMELA) You know him?

(CARMELA *shakes her head.*)

JUANITA: I must leave fine señora, but remember you have an inner brilliance which no one can ever extinguish.

(MANUEL *pushes* JUANITA *and* CARMELA *out the door.*)

MANUEL: *(To* CARMELA*)* You're fired. *(To* JUANITA*)* Never come near this house ever again. *(To both)* Adios!

(CARMELA *and* JUANITA *exit.*)

ALEJANDRA: *(Non-stop, breathless)* Ah oh ay to feel this sensual slinky satisfied again with delicious dreams dancing in my head bare bodies frolicking in fields with a kaleidoscope of colors covering every inch of our sensational skin ay Juan come back to me now Juaaaaaaannnnnnnnnnnnnnnnn!

*(Lights shift.)*

*(A street in the trendy district. Lights rise on* JUANITA *and* CARMELA *on the sidewalk.)*

CARMELA: The new Don Juan?

JUANITA: I spoke the truth.

CARMELA: I'm totally humiliated, totally fired and totally broke.

JUANITA: The old Don Juan left a path of destruction but I leave a path of freedom.

CARMELA: *(Sarcastic)* Wow. I feel so free right now.

JUANITA: *(Amazed)* Lips…she wanted to kiss me on the lips!

CARMELA: So she could rip your clothes off.

JUANITA: Did you see the desire in her eyes, her smile, her joy?

CARMELA: Her insanity?!

JUANITA: Being a new Don Juan can open the doors of the body, mind and soul, chica. I have so much energy pumping through my veins right now.

CARMELA: Almost smooching la señora and now suddenly *you're* her salvation?

JUANITA: Did you see how my words soothed her sadness?

CARMELA: Smooth talking. Grand standing. Love then leave? Where is my Juanita, mi amiga-since-we-were-three, my crazy comadre who runs carefree laughing through the park when we get off work? Where did she go?

JUANITA: She's with Juanito now and together we are bold and brave and bright.

CARMELA: Enough with this let-me-conquer-the world-with-my-new found-machismo-this-momento. We're going straight back to my place. Vamanos...

(ACTIVISTA *enters and hands* JUANITA *and* CARMELA *a flyer.*)

ACTIVISTA: *(Loud, boisterous)* Every single day millions of women are being bared, photographed and displayed on the covers of these magazines in full view for the whole world to see. And billions of these instruments of indignation are sold each day. *(To* JUANITA*)* Would you do this to your girlfriend?

JUANITA: Never.

ACTIVISTA: So you are an enlightened man, amigo, who can then enlighten his amigos who will enlighten their amigos and so on and so on and so on and we will put an end to this, yes the patriarchy is in peril, papi!

JUANITA: No more seduction then destruction.

ACTIVISTA: Continue to be evolutionary revolutionaries compañeros y compañeras. A dazzling new day is dawning and soon the patriarchy will perish!

| DON PEDRO & IGNACIO: | ALEJANDRA: |
|---|---|
| *(Simultaneous)* | *(Simultaneous)* |
| *(Off stage)* Juanita... | *(Off stage)* Juan... |
| Juanita...Juanita. | Juan...Juan. |

JUANITA: Don Pedro...

CARMELA: He wants to kill you.

JUANITA: And Alejandra...

CARMELA: She wants to do you.

JUANITA: A dazzling new day *is* dawning, compañera!

*(CARMELA and JUANITA exit.)*

ACTIVISTA: Chicas unite!

*(Lights shift.)*

*(A leather bar in an industrial district. Lights rise on* TOMÁS, *standing at the bar, in full leather and a harness, holding a beer.* RUFINO, *stands next to him also in leather and a harness with his arm draped over* TOMÁS.*)*

TOMÁS: The ocean is full of fish.

RUFINO: Not all fish swim in our direction.

TOMÁS: You know both directions intrigue me.

RUFINO: Don't remind me. You love inflicting pain.

TOMÁS: Depends on what kind. What's your pleasure?

RUFINO: You don't like my fancy fins?

*(ELENA, in leather, enters, with her arm around her lover,* LEONORA, *also in leather.)*

RUFINO: Chicas, Tomás doesn't love me anymore.

TOMÁS: I'm in the mood to fish.

RUFINO: Torture me why don't you?

TOMÁS: *(Excited)* In the dungeon. Later.

ELENA: You two okay?

LEONORA: They're fighting again.

TOMÁS: To make a point.

RUFINO: And stab me with it.

ELENA: You know you like it. Pleasure and pain, amigo.

TOMÁS: I use my hook and pole but who says they'll bite.

RUFINO: Only I tug on that hook and pole.

TOMÁS: Phylum. Genus. Species. The possibilities are endless.

LEONORA: We don't need to go fishing in the big ocean.

ELENA: We fish in privacy.

*(*JUANITA*, still disguised as* JUAN*, and* CARMELA *enter the bar.)*

TOMÁS: *(Looking at* CARMELA *and* JUANITA*)* Well, amigas, let's cast our nets.

ELENA: Fresh catch.

JUANITA: *(To* CARMELA*)* Don Pedro will never set foot in here.

CARMELA: I don't want to either.

JUANITA: You're with me.

CARMELA: Oh and you'll protect me from them?

JUANITA: Stay just a little while until Don Pedro loses our trail.

CARMELA: I don't like the looks on their faces.

JUANITA: One drink.

*(*JUANITA *walks up to the bar with* CARMELA*.)*

JUANITA: Bartender?

TOMÁS: He's on a deep sea diving expedition. I'm covering. What can I do you for?

JUANITA: Something strong.

TOMÁS: Two stiff ones coming right up.

ELENA: Hola. *(To* CARMELA *re: cigarette)* Got a light?

CARMELA: No...sorry.

LEONORA: Elena, leave the poor girl alone.

ELENA: What? I only asked her for some fire. Jealousy will get you nowhere, chica.

*(*TOMÁS *serves up the drinks in two shot glasses.* CARMELA *and* JUANITA *gulp them down.)*

TOMÁS: Dress code. Where's your leather, ladies?

JUANITA: Ladies?

CARMELA: Leather?

JUANITA: *(Motioning to herself and* CARMELA*)* There's only one lady here...my lady, Carmela.

TOMÁS: I like your look, rich boy.

JUANITA: *(To* TOMÁS*)* I like your leather.

TOMÁS: I swim in both directions.

JUANITA: Leather fish?

TOMÁS: He's smart, this young shark.

JUANITA: Juan.

TOMÁS: Tomás. Elena. Leonora. And this is...

RUFINO: Rufino.

JUANITA: And this is my girlfriend, Carmela.

TOMÁS: Girlfriend?

LEONORA: Right.

CARMELA: He's visiting from the capital.

TOMÁS: The capital? Right.

RUFINO: Visiting? Sure.

TOMÁS: Drop the story.

LEONORA: We've heard them all.

ELENA: You want to check this place out.

RUFINO: So you create an identity that keeps you safe while you shop.

TOMÁS: Or swim.

RUFINO: Watch out for sharks.

*(Techno music comes on the jukebox.)*

ELENA: *(To* CARMELA*)* Dance?

CARMELA: *(Re:* JUANITA*)* I'm with him.

RUFINO: *(To* ELENA*)* You heard the lady.

LEONORA: *(To* ELENA*)* Come on. Side stroke?

ELENA: I prefer breast stroke.

LEONORA: Shall we?

*(*ELENA *and* LEONORA *dance as* CARMELA *and* RUFINO *look on.)*

TOMÁS: You'd look luscious in leather. Chaps, chains, harness. Oh yeah.

JUANITA: Like yours?

TOMÁS: Custom built. The tighter the better.

JUANITA: All studly straps and shining steel.

TOMÁS: Cut the fish talk. Why the drag?

JUANITA: Drag?

TOMÁS: Boy wear. Pants. Jacket. All you need is a mustache.

JUANITA: A little too upscale for this place, I know… maybe you could lend me some leather?

TOMÁS: Chaps, chains, a harness…oh yeah.

RUFINO: *(To* CARMELA*)* Your "boyfriend" is hot.

CARMELA: Thanks. So's yours.

RUFINO: He's taken.

CARMELA: So's mine.

RUFINO: Yeah. Right.

CARMELA: We're deliriously happy together.

RUFINO: I wish I believed you.

ELENA: You have the liquid moves.

LEONORA: When I'm dancing with you…my only partner.

JUANITA: *(To* TOMÁS*)* Your eyes are such an exquisite shade of mahogany.

TOMÁS: Tell me more.

JUANITA: Your heavenly hands travel to exotic locations.

*(*TOMÁS *rests his hand on* JUANITA*'s ass. She rests her hand on his ass.)*

JUANITA: A preview perhaps?

TOMÁS: All depends.

JUANITA: On what we desire.

TOMÁS: Exactly.

JUANITA: Pleasure?

TOMÁS: Pain?

JUANITA: Leather?

TOMÁS: Chains?

JUANITA: Power?

TOMÁS: Passion?

JUANITA: With equality.

TOMÁS: Mutually acceptable. Top and bottom agree that if the flogging fails to fulfill, then it's adios to the action.

JUANITA: So you promote equality over power.

TOMÁS: Water's warm in the dungeon.

(TOMÁS *grabs* JUANITA *and tries to kiss her as the dance ends and* RUFINO *pulls them apart.*)

RUFINO: Watch it, barracuda.

CARMELA: *(To* JUANITA*)* Cariño...we should be getting home.

TOMÁS: He can't leave yet.

RUFINO: She can leave now.

JUANITA: Tomás has a fantastic philosophy of passion.

RUFINO: "All fish favor a flogging with whips and chains?"

JUANITA: He believes two lovers must act passionately on common ground, regardless of prestige or power.

RUFINO: That's it. I'm sick of your fishing around for other lovers.

LEONORA: They always want younger fish.

ELENA: *(To* CARMELA*)* You sure you wanna stay with that stingray?

RUFINO: I come home from a long day at the office and all I want to do is relax with you and some handcuffs, perhaps a whip or two, but you're out swimming in shark infested waters. Fine. Take your fins and find another.

LEONORA: Just like that? You're not going to defend your honor?

RUFINO: Chica, it's not worth it anymore. A man needs affection, love, esteem. Screw honor.

ELENA: Ay, Tomás, you could be a little more respectful.

LEONORA: And you're not doing the same?

ELENA: She's hot but she's not really my type.

LEONORA: Yeah right.

CARMELA: Bueno, amigos, it's been marvelous, really, but we really should be getting home, amorcito.

ELENA: *(To* CARMELA*)* You're curious, aren't you? I can see it in your eyes. You sure you don't want to stay?

*(*CARMELA *clutches onto* JUANITA. TOMÁS *grabs onto* JUANITA's *arm.)*

TOMÁS: Juanito, we can have a dominating and equally powerful time together...all of us. Pansexual pandemonium.

JUANITA: *(Quickly, to* TOMÁS*)* You are worthy of the deepest devotion for your value surpasses any practice of perilous passion.

TOMÁS: Juanito, let's descend into the dungeon, now.

CARMELA: *(Whispering, desperate)* Juanita...

JUANITA: But I must leave and you must stay to find love in your own way.

*(*JUANITA *takes* TOMÁS' *hand off of her, kisses it.)*

JUANITA: Continue to create sacred, powerful, equal space for your lover. With respect. Adios.

*(*TOMÁS *lets go of* JUANITA *as* CARMELA *pulls her away.)*

*(*CARMELA *and* JUANITA *exit running.)*

TOMÁS: Juanitooooooooooo!

*(*RUFINO *grabs onto* TOMÁS*.)*

TOMÁS: His fancy fish talk makes me hot.

RUFINO: Don't you like the way I talk to you, cook and clean for you?

TOMÁS: Why can't you use salty, spicy words like his? The ocean is full of other fish. Juanitoooooo!

(TOMÁS *exits running.*)

ELENA: Love then leave?

LEONORA: Bye bye barracuda.

RUFINO: (*Non-stop, desperate*) And I end up floating alone on my back out to sea, amigas? I need that shark to teach me his liquid lingo and lend me a list of his watery words to wet my whistle oh Juanito por favor teach me Juanito. Juanitoooooooo!

(RUFINO *exits running as lights shift.*)

(*A street in the business district. Lights rise on* CARMELA *and* JUANITA *on the sidewalk.*)

CARMELA: Perilous passion?

JUANITA: He's a gentle giant.

CARMELA: Whips and chains?

JUANITA: Searching for love on equal ground.

CARMELA: He almost dragged you into a dungeon!

JUANITA: Pansexual pandemonium.

CARMELA: Leading us once again into danger…

JUANITA: But see, we swam away.

CARMELA: Barely.

JUANITA: We lingered then we left.

CARMELA: So with you it *is* love then leave.

JUANITA: Not in the way you mean.

CARMELA: Okay, so it's not love, lie, leave, it's love, lure, leave.

JUANITA: Not luring, liberating.

CARMELA: Oh please, you can't change the Don Juan
ways. They still involve luring or liberating, but then
they always end up with the leaving. And where am I?
I'm waving at your "admirers" as we exit, witnessing
their hungry hearts as you make your "escape". I
refuse to be your girlfriend-chica-little lady-significant
sidekick-acting accomplice any longer.

(ROSA *enters wheeling a cart of roses.*)

ROSA: *(Sage-like)* Rosas buy your rosas two for one red
rosas románticas rosas pink rosas simpáticas rosas
yellow rosas  rosas de amistad aroma de amor beauty
for the soul rosas *(To* JUANITA*)* buy una rosa for your
girlfriend.

CARMELA: I AM NOT HIS GIRLFRIEND.

ROSA: Such anger announces the affection you have
deep inside for your señor ay let him buy you one por
favor let your boyfriend show you his affection for his
amorcita.

JUANITA: How much señora?

ROSA: For you a special price two rosas  for the price
of one for I see a softness in your face a tenderness that
says you long to love your señorita mi Roberto buys
me two rosas every day one for love today one for
amor tomorrow.

JUANITA: I'll take two señora.

ROSA: Dos rosas rojas de amor oh there isn't enough
love in this city pues plenty of sexo y plenty of
seductions but not enough true true amor.

(JUANITA *hands* ROSA *the coins and* JUANITA *takes the
roses and hands them to* CARMELA.*)*

JUANITA: For you, querida.

ROSA: Ah look how joyful.

(CARMELA *is not smiling.*)

ROSA: Un besito a little kiss to accompany las rosas.

(CARMELA *glares at* ROSA.)

ROSA: *(Chuckling)* Ay el amor open stay open do not lose the love you long for with las rosas buy your rosas red rosas románticas rosas. *(She exits.)*

CARMELA: Don't start with the sweet talk. I'm late for my next job.

JUANITA: But what if Don Pedro catches up to me?

CARMELA: Charm him.

JUANITA: But Carmelita, you help me navigate through this tricky terrain of passion, privilege and power.

CARMELA: Oh please, you're navigating just fine on your own.

| DON PEDRO & IGNACIO: | ALEJANDRA & RUFINO: |
|---|---|
| *(Simultaneous)* | *(Simultaneous)* |
| *(Off stage)* Juanita... | *(Off stage)* Juan... |
| Juanita...Juanita! | Juan...Juan. |

JUANITA: Carmela???

CARMELA: Ay, the things I do for you. Come on.

(CARMELA *and* JUANITA *exit. Lights shift.*)

(*A church in the business district. An hour later. Lights rise on* BEATRÍZ *getting her photo taken.* DOÑA LOLA *stands off to the side. The lightbulb flashes.*)

DOÑA LOLA: Smile, m'ijita.

*(The lightbulb flashes.)*

BEATRÍZ: Where is he? What if he doesn't come? What will I do?

*(The lightbulb flashes.)*

DOÑA LOLA: Smile. He's coming, cariño.

BEATRÍZ: Of course, he's coming, how silly of me.

*(The lightbulb flashes.)*

DOÑA LOLA: He adores you.

BEATRÍZ: He adores me.

*(The lightbulb flashes.)*

DOÑA LOLA: He worships you.

BEATRÍZ: He worships me.

*(The lightbulb flashes. DOÑA LOLA steps into the picture.)*

DOÑA LOLA: *(Smiling)* If he doesn't come, I'll kill him.

BEATRÍZ: *(Smiling)* Don't murder my husband-to-be.

*(The lightbulb flashes.)*

BEATRÍZ: Ay Mami, no more living alone with los animalitos in our private zoo.

DOÑA LOLA: You've left the life of llamas and lions, m'ija. You'll never be una vieja, an old, rotting spinster, surrounded by exotic creatures living in lonely abandon.

BEATRÍZ: I've dreamt of this shining momento since I was six...to walk up the stone steps to this monumental church and glide down the endless red carpeted aisle of amor with all eyes on me

DOÑA LOLA: And me,

BEATRÍZ: And my flowing white dress,

DOÑA LOLA: my stunning sapphire gown,

BEATRÍZ: my shimmering sparkly veil

DOÑA LOLA: my dazzling designer jewels,

BEATRÍZ: and my glistening golden tiara. Ay Mami!

DOÑA LOLA: Ay m'ija, don't make your mami cry.

*(The lightbulb flashes. DON PEDRO and IGNACIO enter.)*

DOÑA LOLA: *(Turning on a dime, angry)* Late for your own wedding?

BEATRÍZ: Mi cariño.

IGNACIO: Hey.

BEATRÍZ: I was worried.

IGNACIO: I...uh...overslept.

BEATRÍZ: How could you sleep through our big day?

IGNACIO: I was...um...gathering my strength for this...

*(DON PEDRO nudges IGNACIO.)*

IGNACIO: Special day.

BEATRÍZ: So soon we can set sail for a far off isla where we'll lie on a beach, sipping coconut milk from giant straws while we're baking in the tropical sun.

DOÑA LOLA: Vamanos, a few more glamorous fotos. *(To BEATRÍZ)* How's my hair? *(To IGNACIO)* Keep your eyes wide open, hijo. *(To DON PEDRO, sharply)* Keep your sleep walking son in line.

*(The four pose as lightbulbs flash and lights shift.)*

*(A hotel banquet room in the business district. After the wedding. Lights rise as CARMELA and JUANITA enter the reception. CARMELA holds a tray of pastries while JUANITA scopes out the room.)*

CARMELA: *(To JUANITA)* Just stay close to me. Don't do anything. I can't lose two gigs in one day. Got it?

JUANITA: *(To CARMELA)* Sí mi amor.

*(DOÑA LOLA enters and greets JUAN.)*

DOÑA LOLA: Ay y who is this gorgeous man? A friend of the groom?

*(JUANITA takes DOÑA LOLA's hand and kisses it.)*

JUANITA: *(Tentative)* Juan de la Cruz, at your service, señora.

DOÑA LOLA: De la Cruz? The ambassador's son? Ay, well it certainly is our pleasure to have you here, m'ijo.

(BEATRÍZ *approaches them.*)

DOÑA LOLA: *(To* BEATRÍZ, *offstage)* Bea...mira...look who's here...the ambassador's son, Juan de la Cruz.

(BEATRÍZ *enters and* JUANITA *kisses her on both cheeks.*)

JUANITA: Encantado.

BEATRÍZ: Encantada. *(She is smitten.)*

DOÑA LOLA: Ay and mira, look how handsome. Que guapo.

(IGNACIO *enters. At first,* IGNACIO *and* JUANITA *don't see each other.*)

IGNACIO: Bea...

DOÑA LOLA: *(To* IGNACIO*)* Go greet some guests.

(IGNACIO *and* JUANITA *see each other.*)

IGNACIO: And...who's this?

JUANITA: Juan de la Cruz. Mucho gusto.

(IGNACIO *shakes* JUANITA*'s hand roughly.*)

DOÑA LOLA: Why don't you go, niños, while I stay here and entertain our special guest.

BEATRÍZ: *(To* JUANITA*)* Wouldn't you like to lick, I mean look...at five layers of white chocolate, whipped cream almond delight?

JUANITA: Sweet confections for an even sweeter bride.

BEATRÍZ: And on top there's a tiny pink and purple ceramic statue of me and Ignacio. The artist captured my shapely figure. He even painted on my shimmering golden tiara. Ay increible. Come on.

IGNACIO: You show the cake to some more of your friends while I entertain our special guest. Man to man.

DOÑA LOLA: Vamanos, Beatríz.

(DOÑA LOLA *grabs* BEATRÍZ*'s hand.*)

DOÑA LOLA: Oye, Juan…

BEATRÍZ & DOÑA LOLA: We'll be riiiiggghhhht back. *(They exit quickly.)*

IGNACIO: Juanita…

JUANITA: I believe the name is Juan.

IGNACIO: What if my father sees you?

JUANITA: He won't recognize me. These clothes do have special powers. Nothing can get to me.

IGNACIO: He's distracted anyway. He didn't see you, did he?

JUANITA: I haven't seen him.

IGNACIO: Why are you even here?

JUANITA: To congratulate you on your marriage.

IGNACIO: Look, I can explain all of this…this marriage is arranged…and…

JUANITA: I don't care.

IGNACIO: But being with you…it was real, I swear.

JUANITA: And yet there you are and here I am.

IGNACIO: But won't you at least listen to…

JUANITA: Poor Beatriz.

IGNACIO: But I don't feel for her what I feel for you.

JUANITA: She has no idea the lie she's living right now?

IGNACIO: Don't say anything to her. Not here. Not now.

JUANITA: She needs to know.

IGNACIO: My father will kill me and you. I'll work out a way to be with you.

JUANITA: Too late for that.

*(DON PEDRO enters.)*

DON PEDRO: Hard to believe your friend is a married man.

JUANITA: Very hard to believe, señor.

DON PEDRO: Venga, Ignacio, stay close to your bride. Vamanos.

(DON PEDRO *grabs* IGNACIO *by the ear.*)

IGNACIO: Adios, amigo.

(DON PEDRO *and* IGNACIO *exit.* CARMELA *approaches* JUANITA.)

JUANITA: You're working Ignacio's wedding?

CARMELA: That's Ignacio? Ay. Wow.

JUANITA: It's perfect.

CARMELA: Oh no.

JUANITA: We'll just see whose honor is in peril now.

CARMELA: Oh no. No way. You are not doing anything. No confessing. No distressing. We leave once the cake is cut.

JUANITA: You don't need this job. You have many other superior talents.

CARMELA: Don't even start. Yes, I do need this tray wielding payday. I work here. You work in a café. We are not like these people. We sweat for a salary.

(BEATRÍZ *approaches them.*)

JUANITA: Beatríz, I…

CARMELA: Hors d'oeuvres?

BEATRÍZ: Gracias.

JUANITA: You…

CARMELA: Another one?

BEATRÍZ: Mmmm. Gracias. Isn't Ignacio increible?

JUANITA: *(Sarcastic)* Increible.

(DOÑA LOLA *approaches.*)

DOÑA LOLA: *(To* CARMELA*)* Señorita, we need more champagne for the toast. Por favor.

(DOÑA LOLA *drags* CARMELA *away.*)

CARMELA: *(To* JUANITA*)* Don't do anything.

(CARMELA *and* DOÑA LOLA *exit.*)

BEATRÍZ: And are you enjoying yourself?

JUANITA: With such a gracious hostess, how couldn't I?

BEATRÍZ: You're quite lovely.

JUANITA: And you, what a brilliant bride. Your beaming face, your lovely lace veil, your shining tiara...

BEATRÍZ: Really? You like it?

JUANITA: Ignacio doesn't deserve to marry such a treasure.

BEATRÍZ: Do you think he'll be rough with me? I want to please him but I'm scared. I don't know what men want. I only know what llamas, lions and leopards want. I'm afraid of being alone with him.

JUANITA: What do you, Beatríz, desire?

BEATRÍZ: To be loved. Is that too much to hope for? I feel a twinge of sadness though. I'll miss los animalitos. I fear for my new life, away from my parents.

JUANITA: Your perceptive eyes see the goodness in others.

BEATRÍZ: Oh.

JUANITA: Your tender hand holds the truth of their spirits in your palm.

BEATRÍZ: Ah.

JUANITA: Your lovely lips bring hope to their awaiting hearts.

BEATRÍZ: Oo. I feel heat rising up my back, through my chest, around my ears as you speak.

JUANITA: Beatríz...

BEATRÍZ: No man has ever talked to me like this. Men say, "Oh Beatríz, so sweet, silent, special" but they never see inside me like you do.

JUANITA: Beatríz...

BEATRÍZ: Sí?

JUANITA: Ignacio is...

BEATRÍZ: Crazy about me, I know...

JUANITA: He slept...

BEATRÍZ: late today. Hard to believe. But tonight...all that pent up passion...ay I'm so nervous...

(IGNACIO *enters, rushing over to* BEATRÍZ.)

IGNACIO: Cake cutting, querida.

(IGNACIO *grabs* BEATRÍZ *by the waist and kisses her on the cheek.*)

BEATRÍZ: Ay, mi amor.

(IGNACIO *kisses* BEATRÍZ *on the cheek again.*)

IGNACIO: We have to go. Now.

BEATRÍZ: Thank you for your kindness.

JUANITA: Beatríz...I...

IGNACIO: Ahora mismo!

BEATRÍZ: Gracias, Juan.

(BEATRÍZ *and* IGNACIO *exit.* CARMELA *approaches* JUANITA.)

CARMELA: *(Interrupting)* Calmate crusader, you're leaving la fiesta now...

*(BEATRÍZ and IGNACIO re-enter with DOÑA LOLA and DON PEDRO, holding champagne glasses and wheeling in the wedding cake.)*

DOÑA LOLA: Brindis. Brindis. A toast. Don Pedro.

DON PEDRO: Bueno, perfecto...our two worlds are finally one. Beatriz we welcome you to our familia. May Ignacio and Beatríz be forever contentos in all ways. A los novios!

| DOÑA LOLA & DON PEDRO: *(Simultaneous)* A los novios! | JUANITA: *(Simultaneous)* He's a liar! |
| --- | --- |

DOÑA LOLA: Ay, ay, ay!

CARMELA: Juan, do not do this.

JUANITA: *(To CARMELA)* I must. *(To all)* Ignacio does not love Beatríz.

DON PEDRO: Juan...

JUANITA: Last night he slept with Juanita. Maybe tomorrow with Rosita. He's in love with seducing señoritas.

DON PEDRO: Shut him up.

DOÑA LOLA: Let him speak.

JUANITA: Beatríz will lead a lonely life as Ignacio carouses through the city propelled by his...prick.

*(BEATRÍZ screams.)*

DON PEDRO: Lies.

DOÑA LOLA: Por Dios.

BEATRÍZ: *(To IGNACIO)* You desire many women to meet your propelling prick?

*(All eyes on IGNACIO)*

IGNACIO: Well...uh....

DOÑA LOLA & DON PEDRO: IGNACIO?!

IGNACIO: Bueno…I…uh…ay wow…uh…

DON PEDRO: Say something.

IGNACIO: Amorcita, it's just that…

JUANITA: Beatríz is a worthy young woman who deserves to be honored. Cherished. For better or worse. Until death do you part.

DON PEDRO: *(Re:* JUAN*)* Get him out of here.

DOÑA LOLA: Don't touch the ambassador's son.

BEATRÍZ: Ignacio?

DON PEDRO: Hijo?

DOÑA LOLA: Speak!

IGNACIO: Last night I realized that I love one woman and one woman only. And her name is…Juanita.

*(*BEATRÍZ *screams and faints, falling onto the cake.* DOÑA LOLA *slaps* IGNACIO*.)*

DOÑA LOLA: Idiot.

DON PEDRO: Don't hit my son.

DOÑA LOLA: I'll smack some sense into your son. And you allowed this? You allowed this piece of garbage near my daughter? Ay Beatríz, Bea, hija…

*(*BEATRÍZ *comes to.)*

BEATRÍZ: Mami, everything's ruined. My tiara. My cake. My life.

DON PEDRO: *(Re:* IGNACIO*)* Do you believe this imbecil?

DOÑA LOLA: Ay, por Dios, porque m'ija? Why couldn't we find you an honorable hombre…like…like Juan who comes from a fine familia?

BEATRÍZ: *(Caught up in the moment)* I want this marriage dissolved and I want to marry Juan instead.

*(*BEATRÍZ *points to* JUANITA*.)*

JUANITA: *(Back-pedaling)* Oh...uh...not me, señorita.

CARMELA: Confirmed bachelor. He swears he'll never get married.

BEATRÍZ: He's kind to me, Mami. He spoke to me in ways Ignacio never did. Juan sees into my soul.

IGNACIO: You can't marry him.

DOÑA LOLA: Yes she can.

DON PEDRO: No she can't.

JUANITA: For the honor of Beatríz.

DON PEDRO: Screw honor.

CARMELA: We have to leave, Juanito.

*(CARMELA grabs JUANITA as they begin to exit.)*

JUANITA: My deepest apologies señorita for ruining your day but I hope this one ruined day prevents a ruined life.

*(BEATRÍZ tries to exit. DOÑA LOLA holds her back.)*

CARMELA: So sorry. *(To JUANITA)* Now.

JUANITA: Adios one and all.

*(CARMELA and JUANITA exit.)*

DOÑA LOLA: Ven aqui, m'ija. We'll find you another husband and the love and happiness you deserve. *(To IGNACIO)* Vete a la mierda. Go to hell!

BEATRÍZ: I want a kind, tender man like Juan.

IGNACIO: I want a kind, tender woman like Juanita.

DOÑA LOLA: Don't come near my daughter ever again. Shhhh, m'ijita.

BEATRÍZ: *(Non-stop, languishing)* I can never return to los animalitos in our private zoo to the tiny llamas baby lions little leopards where I will lie in loneliness oh Juan...ay cherish and honor me

| BEATRIZ: | IGNACIO: |
|---|---|
| *(Simultaneous)* | *(Simultaneous)* |
| Juaaaannnnnn! | Juanitaaaaaaa! |

*(Lights shift.)*

*(An avenue in the business district. Lights rise on* CARMELA *and* JUANITA *on the sidewalk.)*

CARMELA: Love 'em and leave 'em. Right, Juanito?

*(*CARMELA *tries to leave but* JUANITA *grabs* CARMELA's *hand.)*

JUANITA: Wait...

CARMELA: I can't do this anymore, amiga.

JUANITA: You can't leave.

CARMELA: Because of you, I lost two jobs today. Do you get that? Your crusade cost me cash.

JUANITA: I'll pay you back. Come on. Please? Stay with me. Por favor?

*(*CARMELA *stops.)*

CARMELA: *(Softening)* Look besides the money, I'm tired of the running and cunning and longing I...

*(*JUANITA *kisses* CARMELA's *hand.)*

CARMELA: ...I've witnessed these sad and sorry souls... struggling for survival...

*(*JUANITA *kisses her cheek.)*

CARMELA: ...and it made me feel so lost and lonely and longing for more....

*(*JUANITA *tries to kiss* CARMELA *on the lips.* CARMELA *starts to fall for it and they start to kiss but then* CARMELA *suddenly pulls away.)*

CARMELA: *(Quickly, angered)* Bueno, unbelievable, so that's it? you plant one juicy kiss on me and I'll be under your spell too? ay your newly grown cojones

completely madden me I truly pity "the new Don
Juan" who is worse than the original because this
one is up to the same tricks only with the disguise of
"charisma, compassion, kindness" por favor keep on
saving the stratosphere but don't bother calling me
ever again. *(She exits running.)*

| DON PEDRO & IGNACIO | BEATRÍZ, ALEJANDRA & |
|---|---|
| *(Simultaneous)* | TOMÁS: *(Simultaneous)* |
| *(Off stage)* Juanita… | *(Off stage)* Juan… |
| Juanita…Juanita. | Juan…Juan. |

JUANITA: Don Pedro, Ignacio, Beatríz, Alejandra,
Tomás. Carmelaaaaaaaaa!

*(Lights shift.)*

*(A park in the business district. Lights rise on* JUANITA
*standing next to the statue of Don Juan Tenorio.)*

JUANITA: I can no longer outrace
This lying, love then loss
*(Railing to the sky)*
"Oh Heaven please help me face
The source of this chaos."
*(To statue)*
You created madness
This paradigm of pain
Pleasure to profess
Then solitude again.

STATUE: Screw honor.

*(The* STATUE *steps down off the pedestal.* JUANITA *is
transfixed by the* STATUE's *presence. The* STATUE *pursues
her as she backs away from him.)*

STATUE: Trust my words.

JUANITA: *(In shock)* Ay por Dios…

STATUE: Juanita, you know me.

JUANITA: Are you truly Don Juan Tenorio?

STATUE: In all my granite greatness as I proceed from this need to give your body what your spirit craves, these words, this connection, these caresses that create imprints...

JUANITA: Is this what you said...

STATUE: as your skin senses these signals, leaving the mind apart, and assumes an animal-like existence. My hand to your hip. Finger to face. Lip to neck.

JUANITA: Is this how you talked to all people?

STATUE: Therefore it isn't a legacy of leaving I've created but a need that I've fulfilled.

*(The* STATUE *reaches out and takes* JUANITA's *hand. They dance.)*

STATUE: And so we have...seduction.

JUANITA: Desire.

STATUE: Passion.

JUANITA: Fire.

STATUE: Pleasure.

JUANITA: Bliss.

STATUE: Sí.

JUANITA: More...

STATUE: Seduction

JUANITA: Desire

STATUE: Passion.

JUANITA: Fire.

STATUE: Pleasure.

JUANITA: Bliss.

STATUE: Sí, sí.

*(*JUANITA *breaks from the dance.)*

JUANITA: How could people believe your words?
Where's the equality?

STATUE: That isn't in the equation. I must rise and
dominate to fulfill the natural order of passion.

JUANITA: They were blinded to your truth but *my* eyes
are now open as I say adios to your seduction.

(JUANITA *and the* STATUE *begin to circle each other dancing
again.)*

JUANITA: I tried your tricks.

STATUE: You desire...

JUANITA: And I did enjoy them.

STATUE: passion privilege power.

JUANITA: But your tricks left me trapped in solitude,
emptiness, pain.

STATUE: Such titillating transactions.

JUANITA: I need two equal human beings, walking
forward together, not like you and your conquests, you
galloping away as they sit there, abandoned in the dust
to sift through their lives and try to salvage the savable
parts and sling together some sort of existence.

STATUE: But it was in their nature as it is in yours,
to receive, long for, submit, nurture, not to initiate,
seduce, provide pleasure.

JUANITA: Your attitude and outlook are appalling,
outdated and unacceptable. You no longer exist. Your
ways are history.

STATUE: Let me hold your hand again.

JUANITA: Keep your stone hands still.

STATUE: Let my lips finesse your lovely fingers.

JUANITA: Keep your limestone lips away from me.

STATUE: Let's dance cheek to cheek again.

JUANITA: I am done dancing with you.

STATUE: You say I should no longer exist but you know you have a need for me.

JUANITA: I don't have any need for you.

*(The* STATUE *reaches to grab* JUANITA's *hand. She tries to elude his grasp but cannot and he steps back onto the pedestal, holding her hand.)*

JUANITA: *(Praying)* "Oh Heaven, help me push this piece of polished patriarchy off his pedestal...

STATUE: Powerful prayers...

JUANITA: ...so he can be properly toppled."

STATUE: Such strength from your delicate arms.

JUANITA: Courage now courses through my veins helping me stop your legacy of lost love and lackluster lives.

*(*JUANITA *gives a heave and tries to push the* STATUE *off his pedestal.)*

JUANITA: Return to silent stone.

STATUE: Not until you pay for your sins.

JUANITA: What sins?

STATUE: Gallivanting dressed as a man to try to improve the gender bender battles that transpire, to basically buck the system, status quo, the way things are, should be, will be, forever, and ever amen.

JUANITA: That's not a sin.

STATUE: That's a sin, señorita. Juanita de la Cruz, your time is up and...

JUANITA: Don Juan Tenorio your time is up and over.

*(The* STATUE *suddenly pulls* JUANITA *up onto the pedestal with him.)*

STATUE: One last kiss and your ability to seduce will remain while I leave and return to silent stone.

JUANITA: Then you'll free me to flee?

STATUE: Sí.

JUANITA: If I give you just one?

STATUE: Only.

JUANITA: Quickly.

STATUE: So suavecito.

*(The* STATUE *lifts* JUANITA's *hand to his lips. He kisses her hand lightly. Strange sounds fill the air.)*

JUANITA: Uncanny kisser. *(Beat)* Tiny shockwaves race through my entire body...heightened highways of pleasure and pain...

STATUE: You like this.

JUANITA: No. Maybe. Yes. I definitely shouldn't. Oh I think I do.

STATUE: One more.

JUANITA: Okay.

STATUE: One little kiss, that's all.

*(The* STATUE *kisses* JUANITA's *hand again. The strange sounds grow.)*

STATUE: Un besito más.

JUANITA: So is this where my life ends, kaboom, fin?

*(The* STATUE *puts his hand around* JUANITA's *waist. The strange sounds crescendo. He kisses her lightly on the lips. Silence. She pulls away.)*

JUANITA: Your limestone lips.

STATUE: Turned stone cold. My force fades. My kiss loses its power to do what it usually does.

JUANITA: I've kissed the past adios. One final battle and its farewell to you forever.

(JUANITA *heaves and pushes them off the pedestal.*)

STATUE: So you've toppled me. Your war-like will weakened my wherewithal to woo. What's a stone statue to do?

JUANITA: Adios Don Juan Tenorio. You're through.

STATUE: No passion. No privilege. No power. I am history. Buena suerte, good luck, adios para siempre.

(*The* STATUE *disappears into the stratosphere in a flash of light.* JUANITA, *stunned, stands in silence. A few beats.*)

(IGNACIO *enters running, his appearance is wild and disheveled.*)

IGNACIO: (*Non-stop, breathless, desperate*) I've searched the streets for you I've caroused in bars eating food with my bare hands smoking unfiltered cigarettes drinking glasses of ale and urinating on trees I've I've I've passed out on park benches dreaming I see you reclining in a bathtub as I slide into the water fully clothed yet eager for submersion next to your floating body and awakening to run further search harder to find you.

JUANITA: Ignacio…

IGNACIO: No more high society marriage…

JUANITA: And your honor?

IGNACIO: Screw honor. I've left all that behind to embrace a new adventure with you.

JUANITA: And your father's threat of vengeance…his mission of murderous madness?

IGNACIO: I think he lost your trail as I roamed the streets to find you.

(BEATRÍZ *enters running. She still wears her bridal gown, her veil is askew and torn, her hair wild.*)

BEATRÍZ: (*Non-stop, breathless, desperate*) Juan marry *me* because he will never compare to you I ran away from all of them because they didn't understand the need I have for kindness compassion didn't realize they put me in a tiny sea shell to stare at silently when I am a serpent oh oh oh I dream of tropical jungles with cool oasis pools where we lie together oh how I want to slither and slide with you.

IGNACIO: You can't have her.

BEATRÍZ: Her? No. Him.

IGNACIO: You'll see.

JUANITA: Ay, Heaven help me.

(ALEJANDRA *enters running. Her makeup wild. Her suitcase overflowing.*)

ALEJANDRA: (*Non-stop, breathless, desperate*) Juan let's carouse through the countryside with the tall grass whipping our bare bottoms as we frolic in the fields oh in my dreams our two sensuous selves like little birds soar over a landscape in amber amethyst sapphire ruby emerald with las fantásticas tiny florecitas covering our private parts as the wild wind whirrs past our beautiful bare bodies.

BEATRÍZ & IGNACIO: Another woman?

BEATRÍZ: You prefer older women?

ALEJANDRA: I'm not that old.

IGNACIO: What did you do?

ALEJANDRA & BEATRÍZ: Juanito?

JUANITA: I…

(TOMÁS *enters running.*)

TOMÁS: *(Non-stop, breathless)* Juanito your fancy fish words leave me longing for more why can't we dance off together and descend into the dungeon for some mutually agreeable play with leather toys and girls and boys and all kinds of sensual joy things that buzz things that beep things that take us to the deep whips and chains pleasure and pain so we can get off again and again?

ALEJANDRA, BEATRÍZ & IGNACIO: Another man?

ALEJANDRA & BEATRÍZ: You like men?

ALEJANDRA: Maybe a threesome then?

TOMÁS: *(To* JUANITA *re:* IGNACIO*)* Are you with him?

IGNACIO: I want her to be.

TOMÁS: Which school do you prefer to swim in? Mine? His?

ALEJANDRA & BEATRÍZ: She?

TOMÁS: She. He.

JUANITA: I...

*(*CARMELA *enters running.)*

CARMELA: *(Non-stop, breathless, desperate)* Ay Juanita I dreamt I saw myself inside a wood paneled church sitting on a bench in a crowd of people as I watched you approach me with large brown bird like wings sprouting from your shoulders and I stood up suddenly embracing you as you began to take flight and I awoke in a cold sweat saying "I don't want to abandon mi amiga in the street what if she flies away and I never see her ever again" In fact, I think I actually might want to be with you. Ay Juanita!

ALEJANDRA, BEATRÍZ, IGNACIO & TOMÁS: *(Disbelief)* Another woman?

CARMELA: Get in line.

ALEJANDRA: *(Excited)* Really? All of us?

BEATRÍZ: *(Shock)* Juanita? Carmela? What about Juanito?

TOMÁS: Juanito and Juanita. Chico y chica. Hombre y mujer.

ALEJANDRA: *(More excited)* With women or men is one thing...but...Juanito/Juanita? Ay, ay, ay, I've fallen for a femenino, masculina, tricked-out tranny?

*(EDWINA and MANUEL enter running.)*

MANUEL: No more tricks.

EDWINA: *(To ALEJANDRA)* Come back to us.

MANUEL: *(To JUANITA)* You're ruining our familia.

EDWINA: *(To ALEJANDRA)* Or take me with you.

ALEJANDRA: Juanito/Juanita cares for me more than you do.

*(RUFINO enters running. His apron askew. Notebooks and pens overflowing his pockets)*

RUFINO: Ay teach me Juan, after Tomás ran out I felt so alone I must keep Tomás you must teach me your words por favor?!

TOMÁS: I wasn't running away forever.

RUFINO: For how long then?

TOMÁS: Until I get him/her to join us. Juanito/Juanita?

*(DOÑA ALMA, DON PEDRO and HORTENSIA enter running.)*

HORTENSIA: Papi, Mami, oh we found Ignacio and Juaaaannnnn!

DOÑA ALMA: Ignacio, m'ijo.

DON PEDRO: Ignacio, you are going to come back with us right now.

IGNACIO: But I want Juanita.

DON PEDRO: Juanita? Juan?

CARMELA: *(To* JUANITA*)* Ay, amiga, confess now or forever confuse their lives.

JUANITA: I, Juanita de la Cruz… *(She takes off her hat to reveal her cascade of hair.)*

*(*ALEJANDRA, BEATRÍZ *and* RUFINO *gasp in shock.)*

JUANITA: Lept into bed with him.

ALL: Ay!

JUANITA: Not knowing he was getting married.

ALL: Oo!

JUANITA: Then his familia found us and so I climbed into his clothing.

ALL: Ah!

JUANITA: Where the threads spun their spell disguising me as Juan

ALL: Oh!

JUANITA: So I could retain my honor and escape his papá's pursuit.

BEATRÍZ: Por Dios.

ALEJANDRA: Imposible.

TOMÁS: Increible.

ALL: He's a she!

JUANITA: I reveled in my new role and tried to bridge the divide between male and female, hombre y mujer, to liberate the lothario's legacy and create a new Don Juan. But Don Juans old and new are gone now so we are forever free to seek our own solutions to the sexual circus surrounding us.

BEATRÍZ: I'm startled. I'm moved. And...I still want you.

IGNACIO: I got here first.

CARMELA: Actually, I knew her first.

ALEJANDRA: Hombre. Mujer. Chico. Chica. I need your words of wisdom.

TOMÁS: Juanito/Juanita. I need your fancy fish talk.

BEATRÍZ: Where will you find your solace?

IGNACIO: Whose bed will you belong to?

CARMELA: Whose whistle will you wet?

ALEJANDRA: Who will you fly with?

TOMÁS: Which school will you swim with?

ALL: JUANITA?

JUANITA: I desire...no one.

ALL: NO ONE?!

JUANITA: I know my Don Juan ways
Created quite a craze
But I'm forever through
With this yearning to woo.

I must now seek inside
The self I'd tried to hide
Which now I need to see
The wiser, truer me.

CARMELA: Ay, chica, what's with the poetry?

JUANITA: Now I have a new verse...my thoughts, words with order being restored.

IGNACIO: The rhyme means nobody wins this time?!

BEATRÍZ: What do I do with my emerging emotions?

IGNACIO: What do I do with my lingering longing?

CARMELA: What do I do with my phenomenal feelings?

ALEJANDRA: What do I do with my waxing wanderlust?

TOMÁS: What do I do to with my dungeon desires?

JUANITA: Let your passion propel you forward to seek your own new adventures inside and out.

ALEJANDRA: And so you're leaving us to paint our own portraits?

TOMÁS: Amigos, he is a she and *(To* IGNACIO*)* she was with you but now she is alone and *(To* RUFINO*)* we must find our own way in this city.

RUFINO: Anyone care to go dancing?

*(*TOMÁS *grabs* RUFINO*'s hand.)*

TOMÁS: And fishing? *(To* BEATRÍZ*)* I have some female friends who could teach you some savvy steps.

BEATRÍZ: I never got to dance at my wedding reception and I've always wanted to learn some savvy steps.

TOMÁS: *(To* BEATRÍZ*)* You might like your lace and satin but you will look fabulous in leather and steel.

BEATRÍZ: Leather? Steel? I'm starting to miss the harnesses and halters of the animalitos in my private zoo.

RUFINO: *(To* CARMELA*)* Come dancing with us again.

CARMELA: Juanita, what about your honor, my honor, our honor?

JUANITA: Carmela, you are worthy of a better love.

CARMELA: *(Indignant)* Really.

JUANITA: Lo siento.

CARMELA: I'm outta here.

TOMÁS: Bueno then sí, with harness and halter…

RUFINO: We'll dance and *(To* BEATRÍZ *and* CARMELA*)* you'll woo and…

CARMELA: *(To* BEATRÍZ*)* We'll win love anew.

*(*BEATRÍZ, CARMELA, RUFINO *and* TOMÁS *exit.)*

ALEJANDRA: *(To* EDWINA*)* I'll teach you about soaring.

EDWINA: Does it involve math? I'm really good with digits.

MANUEL: Does it involve martinis? I'd love another stiff one.

ALEJANDRA: Adios, Juanita/Juanito. Watch us soar soar soar into the stratosphere.

*(*ALEJANDRA, EDWINA *and* MANUEL *exit.)*

IGNACIO: Juanita, but what about our new adventure?

DOÑA ALMA: I'm shocked.

DON PEDRO: I'm disgusted.

HORTENSIA: I'm confused.

JUANITA: Adios, Ignacio.

DON PEDRO: Vamanos.

DOÑA ALMA: *(To* DON PEDRO*)* This is all your fault.

HORTENSIA: I miss Juan.

IGNACIO: I miss Juanita.

DON PEDRO: Familia? Now!

DOÑA ALMA, HORTENSIA & IGNACIO: Sí, Papá!

*(*DOÑA ALMA, DON PEDRO, HORTENSIA *and* IGNACIO *exit.)*

*(*JUANITA *remains alone as she takes off her Don Juan suit and shoes so she is left standing wearing only her under garments. A few beats)*

JUANITA: How do I learn to love
And find the center of
My own heart so that I
Can walk, run, leap and fly?

(JUANITA *looks out over the horizon in silence as lights fade.
Blackout)*

## END OF PLAY.

CPSIA information can be obtained
at www.ICGtesting.com
Printed in the USA
LVOW10s0426101017
551841LV00004B/6/P